D1271553

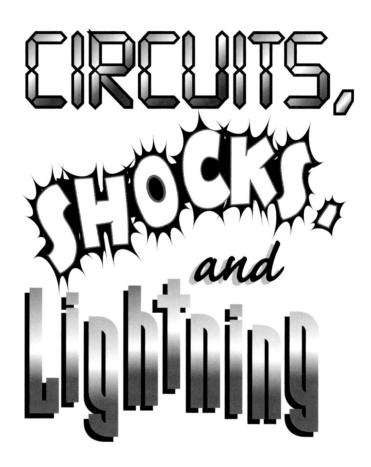

CIRCUITS, SHOCKS, and Lightning

By Celeste A. Peters

RSVP
RAINTREE
STECK-VAUGHN
PUBLISHERS
A Steck-Vaughn Company

Austin, Texas

www.steck-vaughn.com

Published by Raintree Steck-Vaughn, an imprint of Steck-Vaughn Company

Library of Congress Cataloging-in-Publication Data

Peters, Celeste A. (Celeste Andra), 1953–
     Circuits, shocks, and lightning: the science of electricity /
by Celeste A. Peters.
          p.   cm. — (Science [at] work)
     In ser. statement "[at]" appears as the at symbol.
     Includes bibliographical references and index.
     Summary: Explains the different kinds of electricity and describes how
we use electricity every day. Includes related projects and experiments.
     ISBN 0-7398-0143-0
     1. Electricity—Juvenile literature. [1. Electricity.] I. Title.
II. Series: Science [at] work (Austin, Tex.)
QC527.2.P48   2000
537—dc21   99-24771
                                                  CIP

Printed and bound in Canada
1 2 3 4 5 6 7 8 9 0   04 03 02 01 00

Project Coordinator
Rennay Craats
Content Validator
Lois Edwards
Design
Warren Clark
Copy Editors
Heather Kissock
Ann Sullivan
Kathy DeVico
Layout and Illustration
Chantelle Sales

Photograph Credits
Every reasonable effort has been made to trace ownership and to obtain permission to reprint copyright material. The publishers would be pleased to have any errors or omissions brought to their attention so that they may be corrected in subsequent printings.

BC Hydro: page 23; **L. L. Brodeur:** pages 5 top right, 37; **Corel Corporation:** background pages 2–3 and 44–48, 3 top right, center left, 4 center, 5 top left, 6 top, 8, 10 left, 12 bottom, 22, 27, 32 bottom, 36, 38, 40, 42 left; **Geological Survey of Canada:** page 33; **Eyewire Incorporated**: background cover, pages 4 bottom, 6, 10 right, 16 bottom, 17, 21 bottom, 28 left, 29 left, 34, 43; **Sorcha McGinnis:** pages 5 bottom right, 21 top; **Michael McPhee:** pages 5 bottom left, 13, 15 bottom, 28 right, 29 right; **National Museum of Science and Technology:** page 11 top; **Ontario Science Centre:** cover, page 4 top; **Photodisc, Inc.:** cover bottom right, pages 20 bottom, 32 top, 42 right; **Tom Stack and Associates:** page 35; **TransAlta Utilities:** pages 12 top, 15 top, 24, 30; **YVR SkyTalk:** pages 3 bottom, 31.

Contents

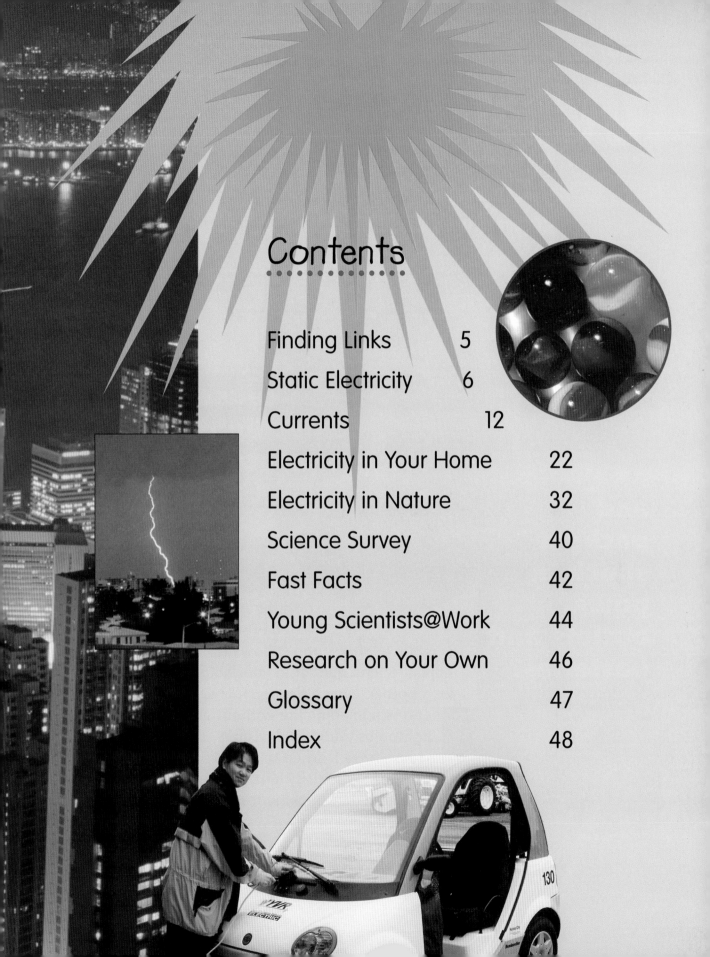

What **makes** your hair stand on end,

causes lightning to flash,

and packs a shock in power outlets and batteries?

Electricity! It is generated in or by your body and clothing on cold, dry winter days. It is created in storm clouds until it is ready to strike, and it flows through every electric appliance and gadget in your house. Electricity can be a bother, even a danger. It is also extremely useful. Can you imagine life without electrically powered lightbulbs, radios, televisions, or computers?

We have learned to capture and control the power of electricity. But what is electricity? Where does it come from? How do we make it go where we want it to go? And how does it work its magic, creating sound in your radio, pictures on your television screen, and heat on your stove top?

FINDING LINKS

Society

We rely on electricity. When the electric power goes off, cities go dark, homes go unheated, and the television goes off! A steady, reliable source of electricity is very important.

The Environment

Electricity pops up in the strangest places. It even comes out of our rivers and waterfalls. Dams are built to capture the power of water and change it into electricity.

Technology

Some of the most amazing inventions of the 20th century are designed to run on electricity. Many appliances around your house plug into electrical outlets or use batteries. The 21st century will see electric cars and other electric wonders.

Careers

Would you like to design computers, robots, electric appliances, or industrial machinery? Maybe repairing appliances or wiring buildings appeals to you. If so, then consider becoming an electrical engineer or an electrician.

Static Electricity

"You shocked me!"

Do you like to "shock" or "zap" your friends on dry winter days, or watch powerful summer lightning storms? Both the tiny shocks at the end of your fingers and the blinding lightning bolts are electricity. Electrical energy is produced by electric charge found in tiny particles called electrons and protons. When electric charge from these particles builds up in one place, such as the end of your fingers, it is called static electricity. Sometimes static electricity goes away, or discharges, little by little, slowly and quietly. Other times it discharges all at once in a powerful display of light, sound, and heat.

What is the connection between electrons, protons, and static electricity?

You cannot see, hear, or feel electrons and protons. Yet these invisible particles are everywhere. They are the basic parts of an atom.

Atoms are the building blocks of matter. Atoms are extremely small. They combine to make gases, liquids, and solids. At the center of every atom is a **nucleus** of tiny particles called neutrons and protons. Electrons are even smaller particles. They form fuzzy clouds around the nucleus.

There is something special about electrons and protons. They carry an electrical charge. Electrons have a negative charge. Protons have a positive charge. Neutrons are neutral—they have no charge.

The electrons of some atoms can move to other atoms and **molecules**. When the electrons move, their charge moves with them. Atoms and molecules that end up with more electrons than protons become negatively charged. Atoms and molecules that end up with fewer electrons than protons become positively charged. These charged atoms and molecules are called ions.

Static electricity is created when you rub certain materials together. Electrons move from the surface of one material to the surface of another material. This leaves many positive ions on the surface of the first material. It becomes positively charged. The electrons build up on the surface of the other material. It becomes negatively charged. These special materials are called insulators.

An Atom

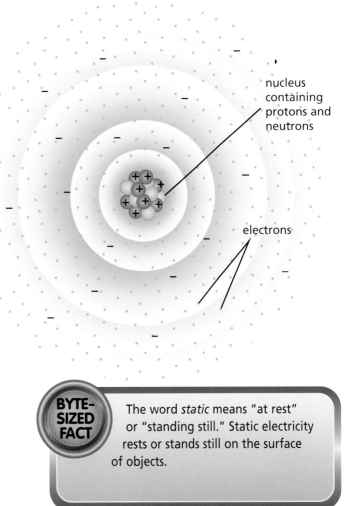

nucleus containing protons and neutrons

electrons

BYTE-SIZED FACT
The word *static* means "at rest" or "standing still." Static electricity rests or stands still on the surface of objects.

Are you an insulator or a conductor?

You are a conductor. You do not know how to lead an orchestra or take train tickets? That is all right. You are a different kind of conductor. You are a conductor of electricity.

An electric conductor is a substance that passes electrons along from one atom to another very easily. Metals such as silver, copper, and gold are conductors. Electrons flow through you easily because your body is made mostly of water that contains many ions. This water is a good conductor of electricity. Pure water is not.

An insulator is a substance that does not pass electrons along from one atom to another. Glass, silk, wool, oil, wax, rubber, and plastic are insulators. They do not let electrons pass through them. Instead, electric charge builds up as static electricity on the surface of objects made from these materials.

> **BYTE-SIZED FACT**
>
> The ancient Greeks discovered that amber, an insulator, can carry an electric charge on its surface. The Greek word for amber was electron. This is where the words "electron" and "electricity" came from.

Conductors

copper

silver

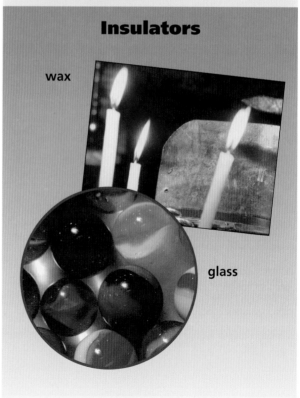

Insulators

wax

glass

Ben Franklin's Shocking Discovery

Today we know that lightning is a flash of electricity, thanks to Benjamin Franklin (1706–1790). He guessed this was the case and did a very clever experiment to prove it.

Franklin decided to draw electricity from storm clouds using a wet kite string as an electrical conductor. First, he made a kite. He attached a sharp wire to the top of the kite. The wire would attract electric charge. Then he tied a metal key and a silk ribbon to the end of the kite string. He planned to stand inside the doorway of a building and hold onto the dry silk instead of the wet string. He hoped this would insulate him from a deadly shock.

A storm arose. Franklin launched his kite and waited. Charge built up in the kite string until its fibers stuck straight out. Small sparks, identical to the electric sparks scientists were familiar with, began traveling down the string to the key.

Now Franklin knew that lightning was electricity. He then invented a device to protect buildings from lightning. To learn how one of these lightning rods works, see page 38.

Ben Franklin was one of the first people to experiment with lightning. His famous kite experiment took place in 1752.

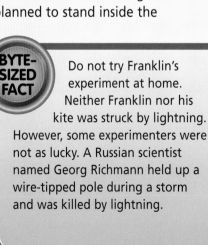

BYTE-SIZED FACT
Do not try Franklin's experiment at home. Neither Franklin nor his kite was struck by lightning. However, some experimenters were not as lucky. A Russian scientist named Georg Richmann held up a wire-tipped pole during a storm and was killed by lightning.

How can you experiment with static electricity?

You can have great fun with static electricity. The following activities will work best on a dry day when there is little moisture in the air. Water is a conductor that quickly drains off static charge.

Sticky Balloons

Rub a balloon in your hair. Now touch it to the wall. Does it stay in place? The balloon has picked up extra electrons from your hair. It is negatively charged. As you bring the negatively charged balloon near the wall, it **repels**, or pushes away, the negative charges in the wall. It attracts the positive charges that are left behind. The negative charges on the balloon are attracted to the positive charges on the wall, so they stick together.

Negatively charged balloons will "stick" to the positive charges on a wall.

Now tie two balloons together with a long string. Rub each balloon on your hair. Pick up the middle of the string and let the balloons fall together. Will they touch? No! They are both negatively charged. Negative charges repel one another.

Crackling TV

Turn on your television. Wait a few seconds, then very gently touch the screen. Do you hear the crackling and feel the tiny shocks? The sounds and shocks happen because electrons jump from the screen to your fingers.

Some objects do not have to touch to allow electrons to jump from one to another. These objects just need to be near each other to exchange electrons.

A Simple Electroscope

An electroscope is a device that detects the presence of static electricity. You can build an electroscope easily. Hold up a length of thread that has a very small piece of cork attached to the end. Wait until the cork hangs very still, then bring an object near the cork. If the object carries an electric charge, the cork should swing toward it. Why? **Electrically charged** objects attract small, non-charged objects, such as hair, lint, specks of dust, and the cork.

If the cork touches a charged object, part of the object's electric charge moves onto the cork and charges it, too. What do you think happens then? The cork will move away from the object because it now carries some of the charge, and is repelled by the object.

Touching the ball on this **generator** can be a hair-raising experience.

The Van de Graaff Generator

This is a metal machine with a ball on top that you often find at science centers and museums. Plastic and rubber insulators rub together inside the machine, creating negative and positive charges. A conductor leads the negative charge (electrons) away from the machine. The positive charge collects on the ball. If you hold onto the ball as it charges, some of the charge escapes onto the surface of your body, charging it. Since all the hairs on your head receive the same positive charge, they repel one another, and your hair stands up.

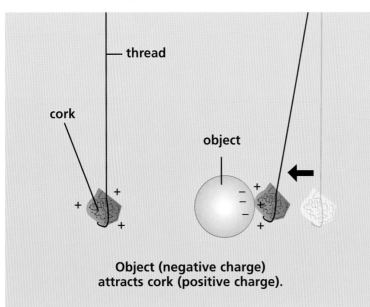

thread

cork

object

Object (negative charge) attracts cork (positive charge).

Currents

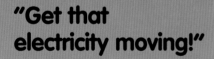

"Get that electricity moving!"

Static electricity is fascinating, but its usefulness is limited. It can also discharge in bursts that are hard to control. If you want to put electricity to work, you need a steady stream of electrons that go wherever you wish. A moving stream of electrons is called an electric current.

Current carries an amazing amount of energy from one place to another. You can turn it into other forms of energy, such as heat, light, and sound. You can even use it to make a magnet!

What creates an electric current?

When electrons move, they carry negative electrical charges from atom to atom. The moving charges are known as electric current.

Electric current flows through conductors. A conductor is a substance that passes electrons from atom to atom very well. Some conductors pass electrons along better than others. The metal copper is a very good conductor. Electrons flow through it easily. Copper wire conducts electricity to many appliances in your home.

Electric current flows through a conductor the way a stream of water flows through a hose. When you put your thumb over the end of a water hose, water pushes against your thumb. You feel pressure. Water in a hose must have pressure in order to move. Electric current also must have this pressure, or energy, to move. The energy that causes electric current to flow is called electromotive force. Electromotive force is measured in volts.

Batteries and electric generators supply the electromotive force that pushes electrons through conductors. Electrons gain extra energy when they are pushed. Electrons can give this extra energy to electrical appliances. Most appliances in North American homes require 110 volts. Some appliances, such as clothes dryers and stoves, turn electrical energy into large amounts of heat. These appliances need more energy. They use 220 volts.

> **BYTE-SIZED FACT**
> The term "volt" comes from the name of an Italian physicist, Alessandro Volta. He was the first person to invent a useful battery.

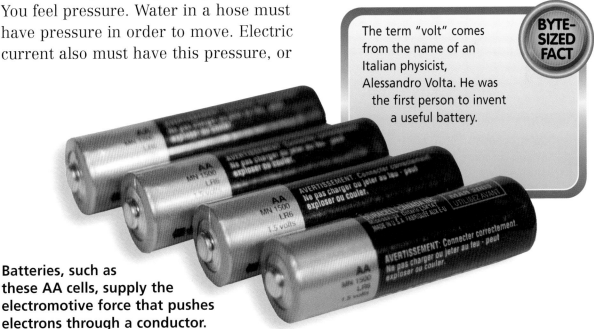

Batteries, such as these AA cells, supply the electromotive force that pushes electrons through a conductor.

What is a circuit?

A circuit is a looped path through which electric current flows. The loop can be very simple, like the wire circuits described on this page, or it can be very complicated, like the circuit board in a computer.

All circuits contain a power source, such as a battery. The power source supplies the electromotive force, or voltage, that pushes electrons around the circuit. Most circuits also contain a switch. When the switch is open (off), there is a gap in the loop. Electric current cannot flow. When the switch is closed (on), it completes the loop and current flows through the circuit.

We often use wire to construct circuits. Wire is a good conductor. Circuit wire is covered by a layer of insulating material. The insulation keeps electric current inside the wire.

BYTE-SIZED FACT

Thick wire conducts electric current more easily than thin wire. Most toys require very little current to run. The wires in their circuits are thin. The wires that carry enormous amounts of electric current from power plants to cities are as thick as your wrist.

A Simple Circuit

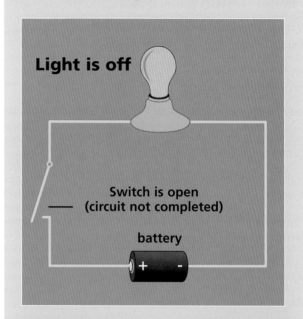

Light is off

Switch is open
(circuit not completed)

battery

+   -

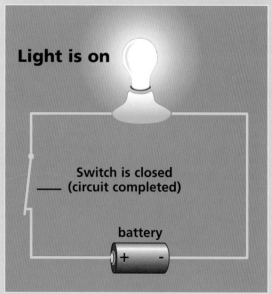

Light is on

Switch is closed
(circuit completed)

battery

+   -

The circuit must be closed in order for electricity to flow from the battery to the lightbulb.

What is resistance?

One way we get an electric current to do work is by placing obstacles in its path. This is called **resistance**.

Electric current flows through some substances better than others. Conductors let electrons pass through with very little resistance. Insulators prevent any flow of current, and poor conductors have a very high resistance.

What happens when electric current meets resistance? Electrical energy turns into another form of energy, such as heat, light, or sound.

This is what happens inside an electric lightbulb. Current enters the bulb by copper wire. It flows through a coil of tungsten wire, then it leaves by copper wire. But not all the energy that goes in comes out. Why? Tungsten has a higher resistance than copper. The energy that the tungsten wire stops from passing through turns into heat and light.

Something similar happens inside an electric burner on top of a stove. As you turn up the temperature dial, you increase the amount of current trying to flow through the burner. But only a portion of the energy that the current carries to the burner can get through. Resistance turns the rest into heat. On the "high" setting, some energy also turns into light, and the element glows red.

When electric current meets resistance inside the wires of a lightbulb, it makes the bulb glow brightly.

Resistance also makes an electric burner glow red.

BYTE-SIZED FACT

Current always travels along the path of least resistance. When uninsulated circuit wires touch, they create a shortcut or "short circuit." If this loop does not include a device that has resistance, too much current flows. The wire gets so hot it can melt or start a fire.

What are series and parallel circuits?

Energy-using devices wired into a circuit one after another are "wired in series." If one device quits, it breaks the flow of electricity. The other devices quit, too. A string of holiday lights that stops shining when one bulb fails is wired in series.

The same current flows through each device wired in series. This means the devices must share the energy carried by the current. When lightbulbs are wired in series, the bulbs glow less brightly than if only one bulb were in the circuit.

Every device "wired in parallel" works as if it were the only device in the circuit. Each device has its own loop connected to the power source. If one device stops working, it has no effect on the others. They just keep working. All the lightbulbs in your house are wired in parallel.

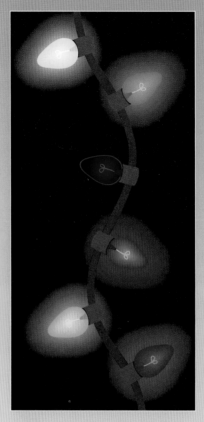

Parallel Circuit **Series Circuit**

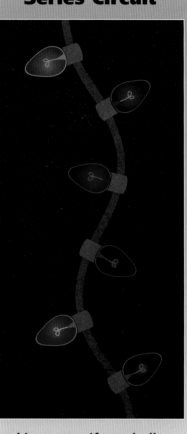

Lights wired in parallel keep working, even if one bulb burns out. In a series circuit, if one bulb quits, all the other bulbs quit, too.

BYTE-SIZED FACT
Some toys need a great deal of energy to run. The more batteries that are connected in series, the more energy there is to run a toy. The battery voltages add up. Batteries connected in parallel do not add up. Instead, they share the work. This makes them last longer than one battery working alone.

How are electricity and magnetism related?

Everywhere a current goes, magnetism tags along. Electric current in a conductor creates an invisible magnetic field around the conductor. You cannot see or feel this magnetic field, but if you put a magnet near the conductor, it would "feel" the field. A magnetic field exerts a force on magnets, causing them to line up with the field.

You can make an **electromagnet** by wrapping a current-carrying wire around a piece of iron. By increasing the current in the wire, you can make an electromagnet become stronger than a **natural magnet**, such as lodestone.

An electromagnet has two poles, just like a natural magnet. One pole is attracted to Earth's north magnetic pole. (See page 33.) This pole is called the magnet's north pole. The other pole

Powerful electromagnets, which can be stronger than natural magnets, are used to lift heavy loads.

is called the magnet's south pole.

Unlike the poles of a natural magnet, the poles of an electromagnet can be made to switch places. Just reverse the direction of the current. North becomes south, and south becomes north.

Electricity and magnetism are related in another way, too. A magnet moving through or near a loop in a conducting wire creates an electric current in that wire. This is called induced current. Induced means "brought on" or "produced." To maintain induced current, the magnet must keep moving. Once it stops moving, the current disappears.

Here is your challenge:

Find the connection between electricity and magnetism in your home! Hold a level compass close to, but not touching, the electric cord or cable of an appliance that is plugged in and turned on. What happens? Does the compass needle move away from its north position? Try this experiment on cords and cables of different sizes, some thin, some thick. Do thick ones make the needle move more?

How do batteries produce electricity?

Abattery is a device that changes chemical energy into electrical energy. Primary batteries are thrown away once all their chemical energy has turned into electrical energy. Secondary batteries can be recharged and used again.

Batteries contain two types of chemicals. One type is in a part of the battery called the cathode. The other type is in a part of the battery called the anode. The chemicals in the cathode try to pull electrons away from the chemicals in the anode. A wall between the chemicals prevents this from happening when the battery is not in use.

A conductive material connects the inside of the battery with the outside at two spots. These spots are called **terminals**. Inside the battery, the cathode touches the positive terminal,

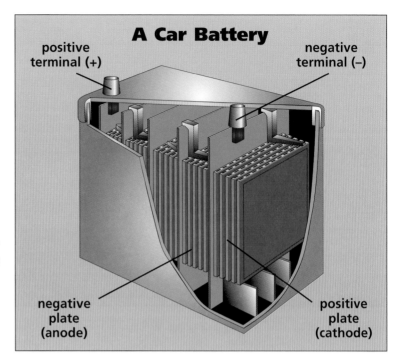

A Car Battery

positive terminal (+)

negative terminal (–)

negative plate (anode)

positive plate (cathode)

A car battery is a type of wet cell.

and the anode touches the negative terminal. When you connect circuit wires to the positive and negative terminals, you make a path through which the cathode can pull electrons away from the anode. The traveling electrons create current. As current flows, the chemicals are slowly used up. When the battery runs out of chemicals, the current stops flowing.

The two most common types of batteries are dry cells and wet cells. All the chemicals in a dry cell are solids. One or more chemicals in a wet cell are liquids. The batteries that power toys and small appliances are dry cells. The battery in your family car is a wet cell.

Here is your challenge:

Find batteries around your house, and identify how many volts they pack. For example, small AA batteries supply 1.5 volts, and square transistor batteries supply 9 volts. What voltage do C and D batteries or the battery in your family car supply?

How do generators produce electricity?

Electric current is also produced by generators. Generators are machines that turn mechanical energy into electrical energy. Generators produce direct current (DC) or alternating current (AC). What is the difference between the two? Direct current always flows in one direction. Alternating current flows first in one direction, then turns around and goes the other way. It does this over and over again very quickly.

Batteries and certain types of generators called dynamos make direct current. On page 18, you learned how chemical reactions inside batteries create current. Inside a dynamo, a coil of wire spins between the poles of a magnet. This creates induced current. But the current itself cannot determine which way to go. The current goes around the wire coil in one direction some of the time. Then it stops and goes in the other direction. A special part of the dynamo, called the commutator, makes all the current flow in the same direction as it leaves the dynamo.

Alternating current is made by a generator that does not have a commutator. This type of generator is called an alternator. Without a commutator, the current that leaves the alternator keeps changing direction.

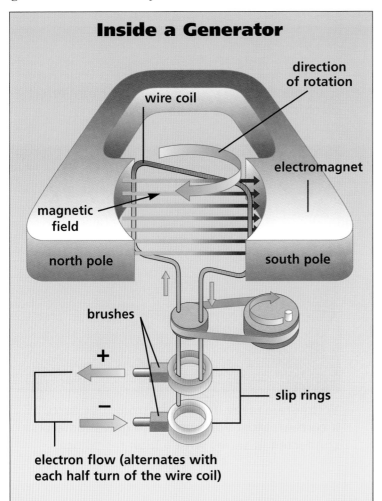

Inside a Generator

wire coil

direction of rotation

electromagnet

magnetic field

north pole

south pole

brushes

+

−

slip rings

electron flow (alternates with each half turn of the wire coil)

> **Transformers** can increase and decrease the voltage of AC but not DC. This is why the current that comes to your house from the power plant is AC.
>
> **BYTE-SIZED FACT**

A coil of wire spinning between the poles of a magnet creates electric current.

How is electric current detected?

A galvanometer is a measuring device that detects electric current. You can make one by winding 50 turns of fine insulated wire around a compass set on a block of wood. Attach the bare wire ends to nails or screws. The circuit you are testing, such as the one described below or the circuit illustrated on page 14, will be hooked to these. When electricity flows, the compass needle moves.

Try measuring an induced current. Wrap fine insulated wire into a coil of about 200 turns. Attach the two ends of the wire to the terminals (nails or screws) of your galvanometer. Now place one end of a strong bar magnet into the coil. The compass needle moves a bit then shows no current. The needle stopped because the magnet stopped moving. To create a steady current, you must keep the magnet in motion. The energy you use to move the magnet turns into electrical energy!

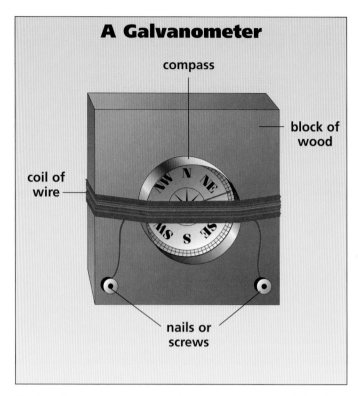

A Galvanometer

compass

block of wood

coil of wire

nails or screws

A simple, homemade galvanometer can detect electric current in a circuit.

Voltmeters measure the electromotive force of a current. Most voltmeters are galvanometers connected in series with a high resistance.

Electrical Engineer

Do you enjoy building electric circuits? Would you like to design a robot? Are you curious about what goes on inside computers?

Maybe you should become an electrical engineer. Electrical engineers invent, build, and operate electric appliances and electronic equipment, such as computers. They also design electrical wiring plans for factories, power plants, office buildings, schools, and homes.

Electrical engineers spend many years studying at college or university. They learn as much as they can about electricity and electrical circuits. They study how electric devices and power systems work. Electrical engineers also learn how to share their ideas and designs in writing and blueprints.

Electrical engineers invent, build, and operate electrical appliances and electronic equipment.

A circuit board is the "road map" for electrical circuits in a computer.

Electricity in Your Home

"Don't forget to turn out the lights!"

Here is a challenge. Can you find a room in your house where electricity is not used? Probably not. Refrigerators, dishwashers, stoves, microwave ovens, toasters, computers, televisions, stereos, CD players, hair dryers, clocks, and lamps all plug into electrical outlets. Overhead lights are wired directly into your home's electrical supply. Power outlets in your garage or on the outside of your house provide electricity for lawn mowers, holiday lights, and snow blowers. We use a great deal of electricity! Where does it come from?

Sources of Electricity

The energy contained in rising steam, falling water, and blowing wind becomes the electricity you use in your home. How? Let's look inside a steam-powered electric generating power plant.

What do we see? Turbines. A turbine is a generator that looks like a huge fan. Steam rising from boiling water pushes the turbine blades around. This spins a giant magnet attached to the turbine. The magnet is inside a ring wrapped with wire. When the magnet moves, it creates induced current in the wire.

Hydroelectric dams and wind farms work in much the same way. The word *hydro* means "water." Instead of steam, a dam uses the power of falling water to turn turbines. Wind drives the turbine fans at a wind farm. A wind farm is a network of several turbines standing side by side in a windy area of the countryside. These turbines harvest the energy of the wind.

Electricity usually leaves a power plant at about 400,000 volts. It travels great distances along power lines made of

The energy in blowing wind and falling water is used to generate electricity.

copper or aluminum. Large transformers at substations decrease the voltage, then send the current to small transformers in your neighborhood. These lower the voltage even further, so it can be used in your house at 220 or 110 volts.

BYTE-SIZED FACT

Power plants use a variety of energy sources to boil water. Some burn wood, coal, oil, or natural gas. Others use nuclear energy or solar energy. Still others get their steam directly from hot water found below the Earth's surface.

Are Electromagnetic Fields Dangerous?

Do you sit quite close to your television or computer screen? Do high-voltage power lines hang above your backyard? Do you chat on a mobile phone for more than 20 minutes at a time?

High-voltage power lines and electronic appliances such as televisions, computers, and cellular telephones all produce **electromagnetic fields** (EMFs). Some people think the radiation in EMFs causes cancer. They refuse to let power companies put up high-voltage power lines near their homes. Many scientists and consumers want health warnings, like the warnings on cigarette packages, put on all mobile telephones.

Other people argue EMFs are not dangerous. They say most of us do not spend very much time near strong EMFs anyway. Therefore, we are not at risk of getting cancer from EMFs.

Some scientific studies show EMFs do cause cancer. Other scientific studies show they do not. Which side do you think is correct? How will you behave around EMFs until science comes up with a definite answer?

"I believe there is more than enough evidence that EMF exposure leads to increased cancer in humans." **Doctor with Washington State Department of Health**

"A link between EMFs and cancer is not only unproven, but rather unlikely." **Scientist who has read over 100 reports on EMFs**

"In my opinion, and in the opinion of many scientists, anyone who uses a mobile telephone for more than 20 minutes at a time needs to have their brain tested." **Scientist who runs an independent research laboratory**

"There is no evidence anywhere in the world that suggests there is any cause for concern over mobile phones." **Spokesperson for Britain's biggest mobile phone company**

How do you feel about electromagnetic fields? Make sure that you understand both sides of the issue before you make your decision.

How does electricity get into your house?

Look around your neighborhood. Can you find the transformers that lower the voltage of electricity that enters your home? In neighborhoods where electric power lines run next to telephone lines, the transformer boxes are high up on telephone poles. In neighborhoods where power lines run underground, the transformer boxes sit on the ground.

If your power line runs aboveground, you can trace its path from the transformer box to your house. At the spot where the power enters your house, you should see a meter. The utility company uses the meter to bill you for the amount of electricity you use in your home.

Once through the meter, the electricity goes to a control panel. The control panel contains small glass fuses or rows of switches called circuit breakers. Fuses and circuit breakers protect your home from serious electrical problems that could cause a fire or shock someone. If too much electric current flows through a fuse, the delicate wire inside explodes. This "blows" the fuse and switches the circuit off.

Finally, wires carry electricity from the control panel to electrical outlets, lights, and doorbells throughout your home.

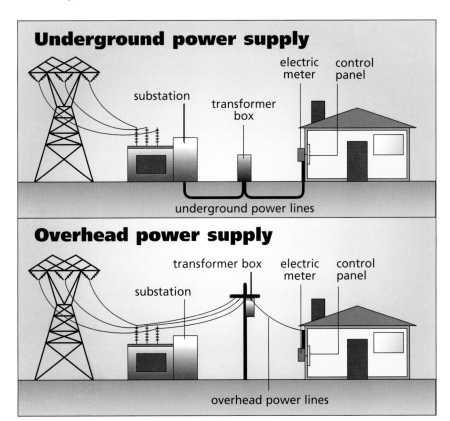

Underground power supply

substation · transformer box · electric meter · control panel · underground power lines

Overhead power supply

substation · transformer box · electric meter · control panel · overhead power lines

BYTE-SIZED FACT

Many large industries need high-voltage currents to run their business. These currents are too high for homes and many businesses. As a result, transformers decrease the voltage to between 110 and 220 volts.

Electricity enters your home through a transformer box on the ground or on an overhead pole.

How does an electric motor work?

Electric motors are very common. They are found in many places. Small motors run household appliances, such as fans, hair dryers, and bread makers. Larger motors run huge machines, such as elevators and building cranes.

Large or small, all electric motors use electric current and magnetism to rotate a shaft. The rotating shaft does useful work. It spins fan blades, gear wheels, or other devices. The shaft has an iron bar coiled in wire at one end. The bar fits between the north and south poles of a horseshoe-shaped magnet. Below is a step-by-step description of what makes the bar and the shaft rotate.

How an Electric Motor Works

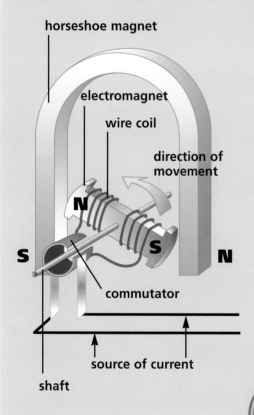

horseshoe magnet

electromagnet

wire coil

direction of movement

N

S

S

N

commutator

source of current

shaft

1. When the motor is turned on, electric current flows through the wire coil. This changes the bar into an electromagnet that has its own north pole and south pole. The north pole of the electromagnet is attracted to the south pole of the horseshoe magnet.

2. As the north pole of the electromagnet swings around and lines up with the south pole of the horseshoe magnet, the current in the electromagnet reverses direction. The electromagnet's north pole suddenly becomes its south pole. The two south poles repel one another. This makes the electromagnet turn a little more.

3. The electromagnet continues to turn because its south pole is now attracted to the horseshoe magnet's north pole.

4. As soon as the electromagnet reaches the north pole, its current reverses direction again. Now the two north poles repel one another. Round and round the electromagnet goes, spinning the shaft along with it.

BYTE-SIZED FACT

You can make a battery-powered electric motor run in reverse. Just switch the wires attached to the battery terminals.

You Said Watt?

What is a watt? A watt is the unit we use to measure the amount of power carried by electric current. Power is the amount of energy carried by the electric current every second. The watt is named after the Scottish engineer James Watt (1736–1819). Watt discovered how to make steam engines work harder and more efficiently. This important discovery helped fuel the Industrial Revolution.

The amount you pay for electricity is based on the amount of energy you use. This is measured in kilowatt-hours. Here is an example. If an appliance uses 1,000 watts of power for a full hour, it uses 1 kilowatt-hour of energy.

BYTE-SIZED FACT

Often, many appliances in your city need power all at once. If the supply of electricity is not great enough to meet the demand, a power outage can result. Everything goes off!

Your electric bill can get big fast. How can you save energy and money? Here are a few energy-saving tips:

- Wait until you have a full load before running the washing machine or dishwasher.
- Buy appliance brands and models that require the least amount of power to operate.
- Turn off the television when you are not watching it.
- Always turn out the lights when no one is in the room.

Businesses can save money and energy by turning off electric lights at night.

What does electricity do inside...

a color television?

Have you ever heard someone call a television "the tube"? The cathode ray tube is the most important part inside every television. Signals come into your television through its antenna or by cable. The cathode ray tube changes these signals into three beams of electrons. When electrons hit the screen, they make it glow. One beam of electrons lights up tiny red dots on the screen, another green dots, and the third, blue dots. These dots, or pixels, are so small that they appear to blend, creating hundreds of colors. Not all pixels light up at once. Some remain dark or less bright than others. This creates images on the screen.

Hair dryers use electricity to run a motor and to make the heat that dries your hair.

Electrons make tiny dots glow to create the pictures you see on television.

a hair dryer?

Electricity does two jobs inside a hair dryer. It runs the motor that turns the blower fan. It also turns into heat as it passes through a coil of wire. This wire is not insulated. If the dryer touches water, electricity can escape and run through the water. If you touch the water, you could get a serious shock. Most hair dryers have a safety device that prevents this from happening.

a telephone?

When you talk into a telephone, electricity carries your voice through telephone lines to another telephone. The sound waves from your voice cause a metal disk inside your telephone's mouthpiece to vibrate. An electric circuit detects these vibrations. It turns them into an electric signal, then sends the signal on its way. At the other end, the electric signal increases and decreases the strength of an electromagnet in the earpiece. This increases and decreases the attraction between the magnet and a nearby metal disk. The disk vibrates, creating sound waves in the air—your voice!

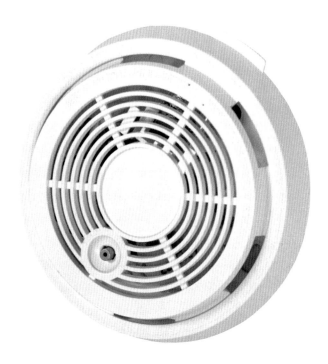

A smoke alarm uses electricity to detect changes in air molecules.

a smoke alarm?

How does the alarm know when to go off? A smoke alarm sends electric charges into the air. If no smoke is around, the charges cause molecules in the air to become charged. If smoke is around, the electric charges cling onto smoke particles. The alarm can detect these charged smoke particles because they move more slowly than charged air molecules. When the alarm senses electric charges that are moving slowly, it signals danger with a loud noise.

An electric circuit turns your voice into a signal that can be sent across wires to another telephone.

Electrician or Electronic Technician

Who put the electrical wiring inside the walls of your school? Who installed the control panel on the jet that just flew overhead? Who fixed your television when it broke? Electricians or electronic technicians did all these things.

Electricians and electronic technicians assemble, install, repair, and take care of electrical equipment. Some follow blueprints to wire buildings. Others help build or maintain the electrical systems in boats, aircraft, theaters, and power plants.

Would you like to become an electrician or an electronic technician? There are two ways to go about it. You can work as an apprentice, a beginner who learns a trade from a more skilled person, or you can complete a training program at a trade school.

Safety is very important for electricians and electronic technicians to learn. They must protect themselves and others from electrical shocks. They do this by following electrical safety codes.

Electricians follow safety procedures to protect themselves from electrical shocks.

BYTE-SIZED FACT

Bare electrical wires can give you a fatal electric shock, even if you do not touch them. Bare wires lying in water send current through the water. If your basement floods, turn the power off before anyone steps in the water. It is also wise to stay away from broken power lines lying on wet ground.

Can electricity power cars?

Good-bye gasoline. Electric cars will fill the streets of the future.

Why? There are two good reasons. First, electricity is a clean source of energy. Driving an electric vehicle does not pollute the air the way a gasoline-powered vehicle does. Second, electric cars are safer to drive than cars filled with explosive gasoline.

Today, every major auto maker is busy designing electric cars. How do they work? Electric motors turn the wheels of electric cars. The motors are powered by batteries or by other devices that generate and store electrical energy. Electric cars also get an extra boost of energy every time they brake to slow down. During braking, the wheels turn the motors! The reversed motors act as generators that send energy back to the storage system.

Electric cars exist today. Why are they less popular than gasoline-powered cars? Electric cars cost more to buy and to operate, but that may change.

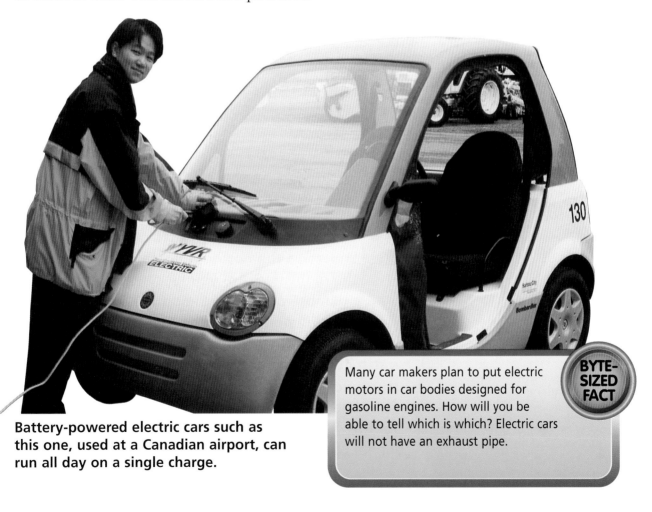

Battery-powered electric cars such as this one, used at a Canadian airport, can run all day on a single charge.

Many car makers plan to put electric motors in car bodies designed for gasoline engines. How will you be able to tell which is which? Electric cars will not have an exhaust pipe.

BYTE-SIZED FACT

Electricity in Nature

"A severe thunderstorm warning has been issued for the local area."

Have you ever seen the **aurora** borealis (also known as the northern lights) shimmer across the night sky? Are you lucky enough to have caught a glimpse of rare St. Elmo's fire? Do you dive under the bed when a lightning storm begins? Electricity in nature is interesting, fun, even scary to watch. It is the source of a giant magnetic field that surrounds Earth. It serves as a weapon for certain fish. And, most importantly, it is a vital ingredient for life. If electrical energy did not exist, human and animal bodies could not function!

What creates the magnetic field in Earth's core?

Deep beneath your feet, in the core of Earth, is a giant generator. This is not a human-made machine. It is a natural generator. It creates electric current and a magnetic field that reaches far out into space.

How does it work? The Earth's core is primarily made of the metal iron. The core is solid at the center and liquid around the outside. The liquid layer is where the generator exists. Inside this layer, molten iron moves around in huge circles. The moving iron carries charged particles along with it. These moving charged particles create strong electric currents within Earth's core.

Electric current always has a magnetic field around it. The magnetic field created by Earth's generator pops out of our planet in a straight line at two points. These points are called the north and south magnetic poles. The magnetic poles move around very slowly. Currently, they are located more than 600 miles (1,000 km) from the Earth's geographic poles. In 1999 the north magnetic pole was in northern Canada, near the northwest corner of Ellef Ringnes Island. It moves northwest 9.3 miles (15 km) every year.

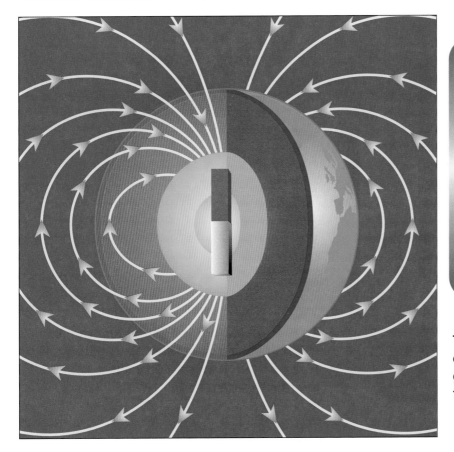

Over hundreds of thousands of years, the electric current in Earth's generator changes direction. The magnetic field reverses at the same time. If this happened today, the needle on your compass would point south instead of north.

BYTE-SIZED FACT

The magnetic field created by Earth's generator reaches far into outer space.

Do you have electricity in your body?

Absolutely! It is called bioelectricity. Do not worry, this electricity is not strong enough to hurt you. In fact, it is very useful. You could not live without it.

Cells in your body act like tiny batteries. Chemicals inside them make and store electrical energy. Your body uses this bioelectricity to do many important things. When you touch, see, or hear something, electric signals run through your nervous system to tell your brain. Likewise, when your brain wants your muscles to move, it sends them electric signals. One of the most important muscles is your heart. The electric signals given off by a beating heart can be detected by a machine called an **electrocardiograph**. Doctors use this machine to detect electrical problems that may be symptoms of heart disease.

Bioelectric signals travel very quickly through your body. They give you the ability to respond quickly when you sense danger.

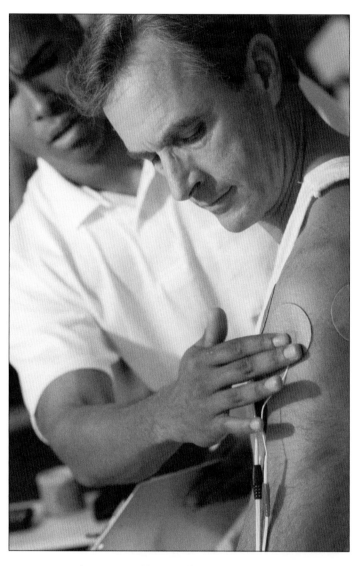

An electrocardiograph can detect signals through electrodes placed on the body. These electrical signals give clues about the health of a person's heart.

BYTE-SIZED FACT
The electric signals inside your body are very weak. They are measured in microvolts and millivolts. A microvolt is one-millionth of a volt. A millivolt is one-thousandth of a volt.

Shocking Fish

This is truly a shocking tale. Actually, "tail" is more accurate.

Everyone has heard of electric eels. Did you know there are electric catfish and electric rays, too? These strange fish look nothing alike, yet they all have one thing in common. All three can produce an electric shock strong enough to stun a human.

Electric eels, which are related to harmless minnows and goldfish, live in the waters of slow-moving South American rivers. These long, skinny fish have special organs in their tails that produce shocks of up to 650 volts. Electric catfish create up to 450 volts in a jellylike layer beneath their skin. The disk-shaped bodies of electric rays have electric organs at each side of the head.

These fish use electricity to stun prey and to fend off attackers. They also "see" with electricity, in the same way that bats "see" with sound. This sense helps electric fish detect prey and nearby objects.

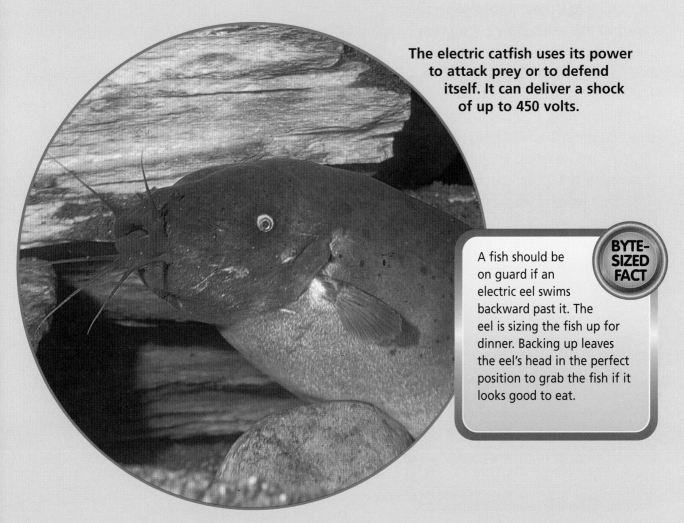

The electric catfish uses its power to attack prey or to defend itself. It can deliver a shock of up to 450 volts.

BYTE-SIZED FACT

A fish should be on guard if an electric eel swims backward past it. The eel is sizing the fish up for dinner. Backing up leaves the eel's head in the perfect position to grab the fish if it looks good to eat.

What is lightning?

Lightning is a great discharge of static electricity that happens in the blink of an eye. What creates the static charge? Strong updrafts inside thunderclouds lift water droplets through the air. The moving droplets rub the air and build up an electric charge, just as clothes tumbling in a dryer create static electricity.

Air is a good insulator, but at some point, it can no longer resist the amount of charge that has built up in the cloud. The air gives way, and electrons dash either from the cloud to the ground or to another cloud. This causes the giant spark and loud thunderclap that you see and hear during a storm.

Ball lightning is a mysterious glowing sphere of orange, red, blue, or white light. It appears immediately before, during, or after an electrical storm. Some scientists believe ball lightning is a form of electricity. Others disagree. The truth is, no one knows what it is.

Sometimes ball lightning comes down from the sky and floats outside. Other times it forms inside houses and planes. People have even seen it pass through walls and windows. It is harmless indoors. Outdoors, it can disappear in a violent explosion.

A flash of lightning between a cloud and the ground can be up to 9 miles (14 km) long.

BYTE-SIZED FACT
It is estimated that ball lightning has been seen by 5 percent of Earth's population. In other words, one person out of 20 has seen this strange sight.

What are sprites and auroras?

Sprites are flashes of light that occur high above thunderclouds. Electrons moving upward from the cloud tops cause sprites. These electrons are speeding toward the **ionosphere**. The ionosphere is a special layer of air that surrounds Earth. It consists of ions and free electrons. This makes it a good conductor of electricity, just like the ground. During a severe thunderstorm, electrons in the top of the clouds are drawn toward the ionosphere in much the same way as a powerful lightning bolt is drawn toward the ground. On the way up, some electrons bump into molecules of oxygen and other gases in the air. The molecules glow and cause sprites to appear.

The Sun sends charged particles into space. Some of these particles head toward our planet. The stream of charged particles is known as solar wind. When the particles arrive, Earth's magnetic field traps them and guides them toward the north and south magnetic poles. There, they enter the atmosphere and bump into gas molecules in the air.

The molecules absorb energy from the charged particles and use it to make light. Oxygen molecules at the top of the atmosphere glow red. Lower down, they glow a bright yellow-green. Nitrogen molecules glow blue or red. They make the purplish-red borders of auroras.

Charged particles from the Sun collide with gas molecules to form colorful auroras.

Auroras are seen most often in the nighttime sky near Earth's north and south magnetic poles. This makes the Canadian Arctic the best location in the Northern Hemisphere from which to view auroras.

BYTE-SIZED FACT

Lightning Rods

Lightning always travels the path of least resistance between a cloud and the ground or from cloud to cloud. Sometimes this means taking a shortcut through good conductors, such as tall trees, buildings, and people.

People can protect themselves by taking cover when a storm approaches. (See page 41 for lightning safety tips.) Trees have to stay where they are and take their chances. What about houses? Many have built-in protection against lightning, thanks to Benjamin Franklin, the inventor of the lightning rod.

A lightning rod is a metal pole on the roof that points up into the sky. A copper wire runs from the lightning rod to another metal rod stuck in the ground.

This protects the house in two ways. First, it slowly releases into the air the positive electric charge that builds up on the ground during a storm. This helps neutralize the negative charge that builds up in the clouds. If there is no difference in charge between the clouds and the ground, there will be no lightning. Second, if lightning does strike, the lightning rod directs the bolt through the metal wire to the ground. This saves the house from catching fire.

BYTE-SIZED FACT Few houses in cities have lightning rods. Metal streetlight poles do the job instead.

A tree growing close to a house can act as a lightning rod, protecting the house from damage.

Have you seen St. Elmo's fire?

It is dark. Storm clouds are building. You hurry down the street, hoping to get home before the rain begins to pour. Suddenly, you notice an eerie green glow on top of a pointed church tower. It is crackling and hissing.

Should you panic? No! What you are seeing is St. Elmo's fire. Consider yourself fortunate. Few people get the chance to witness this rare sight. When ancient sailors saw the green glow of St. Elmo's fire on top of a pointed ship mast, they looked on it as a sign of good luck.

What is St. Elmo's fire? It is an electrical phenomenon. The scientific name for St. Elmo's fire is corona discharge. Objects that have sharp points or sharp edges act as lightning rods. Positively charged particles build up on their surfaces and repel one another off the points and edges when it gets too crowded. This fills the surrounding air with positively charged particles that attract nearby negatively charged electrons. As this happens, gas molecules in the air glow green.

Elmo comes from Erasmus, the patron saint of Mediterranean sailors. Sailors who see St. Elmo's fire consider it a sign of good luck.

BYTE-SIZED FACT
Unlike lightning, St. Elmo's fire is a harmless display of electricity. It does not burn, electrocute, or explode objects it touches. If a storm is building, however, do not stop to admire St. Elmo's fire. Take cover.

Do you know what to do in a lightning storm? Many people are hurt or killed every year because they do not know how to protect themselves. The Lightning Safety Group, an association of lightning experts in the United States, has published safety guidelines. Some of their advice might surprise you.

What are your answers?

1. Should you take cover in a safe place when you first see lightning or hear thunder?

2. Is it safe to be in a car or bus during a lightning storm?

3. Are picnic shelters or baseball dugouts safe places to be?

4. Should you take a shower during a lightning storm?

5. Is it safe to talk on the telephone with a friend during the storm?

An open picnic area is not a safe place to stay when a lightning storm starts.

Survey Results

By the time you see lightning or hear thunder, you are already in danger. Take cover as soon as high winds or dark clouds show up. Do not go back out too soon. You are still at risk 30 minutes after the last crash of thunder. Large buildings are the safest places to take cover. Cars and buses are safe, too, as long as you keep the windows rolled up and you do not touch metal surfaces. Open areas, including baseball dugouts and picnic shelters are not safe. Lightning can harm you even if you are at home. Do not touch conductors that lead outside, such as wires or plumbing. This means you should not talk on the telephone, take a shower, or work at a computer terminal during a storm. You also have a good excuse not to do the dishes!

Here is your challenge:

Look around your community. Identify safe places to take cover when a lightning storm heads your way. At the park, where is the nearest enclosed shelter? How long would it take you to get to the shelter if you ran? Where else do you spend a lot of time outdoors? Can you identify a good shelter nearby?

Fast Facts

1. When you build up static electric charge on your body by walking across carpet on a dry day, you leave behind invisible footprints of the opposite electric charge.

2. Lightning strikes somewhere in the world about 100 times every second.

3. Lightning does not occur just where it is raining. It can strike up to 10 miles (16 km) away.

4. Spacecraft have detected lightning high in the atmosphere of the planet Jupiter.

5. When volcanoes erupt, the particles in the ash cloud rub together and produce static electricity. This creates volcanic lightning.

6. Birds sitting on electric wires do not get electrocuted. They are safe because they do not touch the ground or any other object. There is no way for electricity to flow through them to the ground.

7. People often leap across the room when they get an electric shock. The electricity contracts certain muscles very quickly, making them jump.

8. Some countries use 220 volts for all their appliances instead of 110 volts.

9. St. Elmo's fire can be seen glowing around ship masts, the propellers and wings of planes, and even the horns of cattle.

10. Some electric cables are covered in metal. The metal protects nearby objects from the electromagnetic field the electricity produces.

11. A tiny silicon computer chip contains millions of electronic components.

12. The alternating current that runs appliances in North American homes changes its direction of flow 120 times per second.

13. The lowest edges of auroras are at least 40 miles (64 km) above Earth. That is higher than jet airplanes fly.

14. Most lightning bolts are 7 to 10 miles (11 to 16 km) long.

15. A quartz crystal creates a small amount of electric current when it is squeezed or stretched. This is known as the piezoelectric effect. Some barbecue lighters make an electric spark this way.

16. A type of battery called a solar cell, or photovoltaic cell, changes sunlight into electricity. Solar cells are very important energy sources for satellites in orbit around Earth.

17. If the electric signals that tell your heart when to beat stop working properly, a human-made electronic device can do the job. The device, called a pacemaker, sends electric signals to your heart at a steady rate or pace.

18. Long, skinny **fluorescent lightbulbs** use only one-eighth the electricity **incandescent** lightbulbs use. They also last much longer.

19. Metals and some ceramic materials lose their resistance to electric current at very low temperatures. They become **superconductors**.

20. A Danish scientist named Hans Christian Orsted discovered the relationship between electricity and magnetism in 1819.

Young Scientists@Work

Test your knowledge of electricity with these questions and activities. You can probably answer the questions using only this book, your own experiences, and your common sense.

FACT: Electric current travels most easily through conductors. Insulators do not let current pass through.

TEST: Which of the following materials are conductors of electricity? Which are insulators?

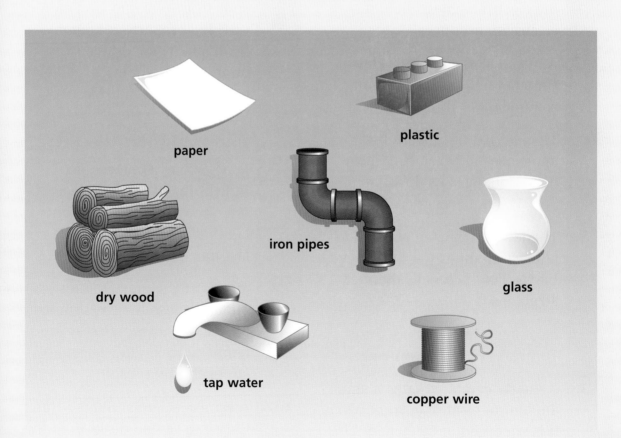

paper

plastic

dry wood

iron pipes

glass

tap water

copper wire

Answers: paper (insulator), plastic (insulator), wood (insulator), iron pipes (conductors), glass (insulator), tap water (conductor), copper wire (conductor).

FACT: You can change the strength of an electromagnet by changing the amount of electric current flowing through it.

TEST: Experiment by building your own electromagnet. Wrap several turns of insulated wire around an iron nail, and connect the wire ends to the poles of a battery. (Note: Put an energy-using device, such as a lightbulb, somewhere in your circuit to avoid creating a short circuit.) The iron nail becomes an electromagnet. Count how many pins or metal paper clips your electromagnet can lift. Wrap more turns of wire around the nail. Count the number it can pick up now.

PREDICT: Will your electromagnet get stronger or weaker as you add more turns of wire? Look back to page 17 if you need a clue.

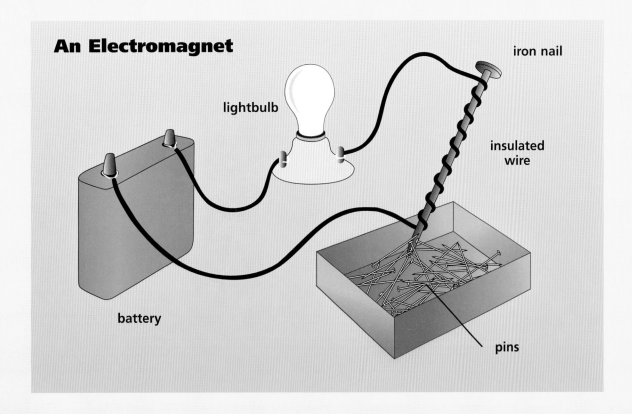

An Electromagnet

iron nail

lightbulb

insulated wire

battery

pins

Research on Your Own

There are many places to learn more about the science of electricity. Your local library, electric utility company, and the Internet all have excellent information for you. Here are some awesome resources to try.

Great Books

Bartholomew, Alan. *Electric Gadgets and Gizmos: Battery-Powered Buildable Gadgets that Go!* Toronto: Kids Can Press, 1998.

Harper, Suzanne. *Sheets, Streaks, Beads, and Balls: Lightning.* New York: Franklin Watts, 1997.

Hooper, Tony. *Electricity.* Austin, TX: Raintree Steck-Vaughn Publishers, 1994.

Shepherd, Donna Walsh. *Light Shows in the Night Sky: Auroras.* New York: Franklin Watts, 1995.

Tomecek, Steve. *Simple Attractions: Phantastic Physical Phenomena™.* New York: W.H. Freeman and Company, 1995.

Great Websites

Beakman's Electric Motor
http://fly.hiwaay.net/~palmer/motor.html

Child's Guide to Electric Safety
www.ladwp.com/resserv/safety/chldsafe.htm

Energy Quest
www.energy.ca.gov/education/

Kids' Lightning Information and Safety
www.azstarnet.com/~anubis/zaphome.htm

Glossary

aurora: A natural display of light that appears in the sky above Earth's north and south poles. When seen in the north, the aurora is known as the northern lights.

electrically charged: Carrying a positive or negative electrical charge

electrocardiograph: A machine that detects the electric signals given off by a beating heart. It draws a line on a piece of paper. Every time a beat comes along, it makes a bump in the line. Cardio means "heart," and "graph" refers to the drawing.

electromagnet: A magnet created when electric current flows around an iron object

electromagnetic field: A space in which electromagnetic radiation exists. This type of radiation includes ultraviolet light, visible light, infrared rays (heat), radio waves, gamma rays, X rays, and microwaves.

fluorescent lightbulb: A light that has a gas inside it. The gas passes energy from electric current to a layer of material on the inside of the bulb and makes it glow.

generator: A machine that changes mechanical energy into electric energy

incandescent: Glowing from heat; for example, when electric current meets resistance in a conductor

ionosphere: A layer of Earth's atmosphere in which a large portion of the atoms and molecules are electrically charged

molecule: A tiny particle made of two or more atoms bound together

natural magnet: Specific elements that act like tiny magnets. When these elements are aligned, it is a permanent magnet.

nucleus: The core of protons and neutrons at the center of an atom

repel: Push away from

resistance: The ability of a material to convert energy carried by a current into such products as light or heat. Resistance is measured in units called ohms.

superconductor: A conductor that offers little, if any, resistance to the flow of electric current

terminal: The part of a battery that electricity flows out of or in to

transformer: A device that increases or reduces the voltage provided by a power line. Transformers can be used only with alternating current.

Index